LEYSEII JOHNSTON

ADVERTISING

HOW WE RAN A BOUTIQUE AGENCY | 1972 - 1990

LEYSEN JOHNSTON

ADVERTISING

HOW WE RAN A BOUTIQUE AGENCY | 1972 - 1990

"Advertising is fundamentally persuasion
and persuasion happens not to be a science but an art."
- William Bernbach

MARK LEYSEN

TSP

TRAVELING SHOES PRESS
PO BOX 332
Pioneertown, CA 92268

Leysen Johnston Advertising: How We Ran A Boutique Agency | 1972-1990
ISBN# 978-1-0881-5661-2

© 2023 Mark Leysen

Book design by Jon Christopher
Editing by Russ Sacco

To an enduring partnership

CONTENTS

NOT YET THIRTY

In 1972, after two years at a small ad agency in Garden Grove, I got fired and found myself without a job. I'd been canned over a dispute with the creative director and knew I was not about to get a letter of recommendation.

I mentioned my new jobless status to my friend Steve Johnston whom I'd known since high school, and he suggested that we should start our own agency, because he'd just quit his job as a DJ. He had a degree in radio and television broadcasting from Long Beach State University, and I had a degree in art from Cal State Fullerton University.

On the face of it, it seems pretty straightforward that there are only two ingredients required to start an ad agency: that is a copywriter, and an art director. As someone in the ad business once said, "Nothing good comes from more than three people in a room."

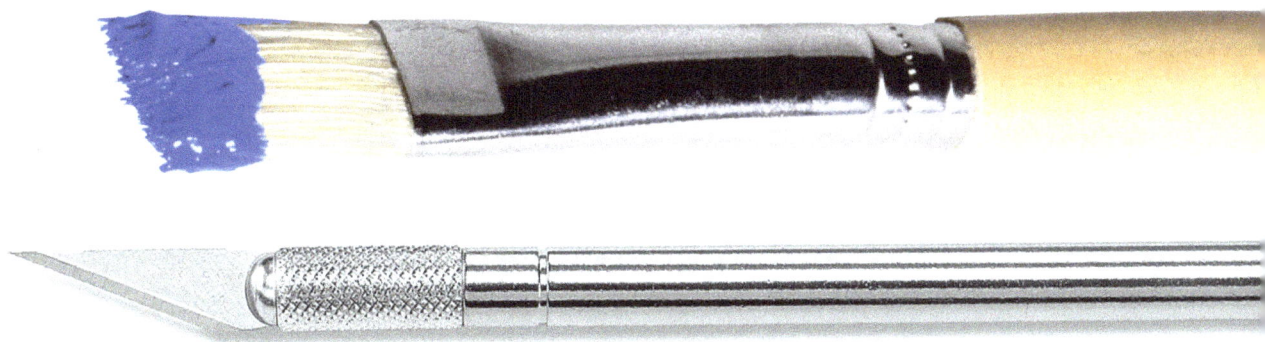

Steve would be the copywriter and I'd be the art director. As is dramatically pointed out on the hit series *Mad Men*, art follows copy. After a bit of brainstorming, Steve would write out a punchy headline and sub head, and I'd create the art to graphically drive the point across. It was a simple solution. All we needed was an office and clients.

Both of us were 29 years old and as the cliche of the times went, "Don't trust anyone over thirty." We'd both remain 29 in our hearts and minds for the next eighteen years. It helps to have a young attitude in advertising.

CHOOSING A NAME

We found a small one-room space in Newport Beach that rented for $80 a month, and we split the total. As partners we would also split all income 50/50 from the onset, and it would remain that way for the duration of our partnership.

Originally we started out as Advantage Advertising, but several months later we got a "Cease and Desist" letter from an attorney representing an agency with the identical name. We tried various combinations with the word "Ad" in it, but came up blank. A friend suggested we use our last names, because certainly no one could sue us over that.

When it came to the big agencies, certainly some of the most famous New York ad firms did just that, using a combination of the partners last names like: Doyle Dane Bernbach, McCann Erickson, Ogilvy & Mather, or a singular name like J. Walter Thompson, and Leo Burnett in Chicago.

We settled on Leysen/Johnston and years later incorporated and added Inc. to make us look more substantial.

HUSTLING FOR CLIENTS

In need of work, I scanned the local newspaper and responded to an "illustrator" Wanted Ad. I got the job drawing cartoon frogs that were silk screened on throw pillows sold through various gift shops and boutiques. It was my first paycheck that netted me $700, and although Steve was not involved, half went to him, and we were in business.

Steve at one time hosted an evening radio show on KOCM, a local FM station broadcast out of Newport Beach. Later, he would pitch the owner, and we ended up having them as an early client. He also approached **Coast Music**, a retail outlet for all kinds of musical instruments and got them as a client.

Above: Logo design and newspaper ad depicting the original Balboa Pavilion

A few doors down from our office, two women had set up an early version of Planned Parenthood, called **Apcare**. They counseled young women who had an unwanted pregnancy with the obvious three choices; 1. Have the baby 2. Put it up for adoption, or 3. Have an abortion.

To advertise their service we created an ad, but the local newspaper wouldn't accept it for being "too controversial."

So I enlarged the ad and turned it into a poster, which was placed in college campuses, record and gift shops, or wherever the younger demographic hung out. We submitted the poster to an annual advertising awards function, and it won first place in the poster category.

Over the years, we won many advertising awards, which we framed and hung in our entry lobby to impress clients.

Another neighbor in the building was the head of the **San Joaquin Refining** company who we got to know when we pigeonholed him on his daily smoking sessions outside the office. (His secretary wouldn't let him smoke inside.) We showed him samples of our work, and soon we were involved in creating a glossy duotone brochure for the company's products.

SAN JOAQUIN REFINING

Steve, in general, wore two hats. He also went out and hustled for new clients, which in ad speak was called an account executive. One day he cold-called a new Mexican restaurant ready to open called **Mi Casa**, and set up a meeting with the owner who definitely wanted to advertise.

Steve's introductory headline for **Mi Casa** was, "Our Meals are a Trip to Mexico." I chose the typeface for the restaurant logo, placed it inside of a Spanish tile roof, and also created a cartoon mascot of a burro drinking a margarita, and designed the menu. We did many print ads for **Mi Casa**, most on the lighter somewhat humorous side, and they remained our client for many years. Several of the ads framed by the owner and hung in the entry lobby are still on display to this day nearly 50 years later.

PSST! WANT TO GUACAMOLE?

You don't have to go across the border to guacamole anymore. The secret is out at Mi Casa.

It was during the Mexican Revolution that a Federale Pilot bombed a small village with what he thought was explosives, but turned out to be a ton of ripe avocados.

All of Mexico and much of North America now remember this tasteful event as one of the most delicious, if not the messiest in current history.

Mi Casa is fortunate to have the rights to this original recipe. Now you can really guacamole the way you've always wanted to.

Our hats are on to that misguided pilot. Now, when you want to guacamole you can at Mi Casa. Remember, our meals are a trip to Mexico — it's a trip worth taking.

MI CASA
MEXICAN RESTAURANT
296 E. 17th St.
COSTA MESA ● HILGREN SQUARE
Open Daily at 11:00 a.m. ● Phone 645-7626

BANKAMERICARD, MASTERCHARGE and AMERICAN EXPRESS

STEALING A CLIENT

While stealing a client may seem a bit unethical, it certainly isn't illegal, and it happens between agencies.

When I was still working for the Garden Grove ad agency, the owner let me have direct contact with one client, which was unusual since most jobs were handed down to me by the art director, and I had no idea who originated the job. In this case it was **Westab**, a paper company. The marketing director I worked with was in charge of their division that specialized in producing school supplies. This included note pads, journals, three-ring binder covers, packaging, labels, and slip sleeves for an assortment of materials.

Below: to drive the point across - I drew every kind of pen imaginable.

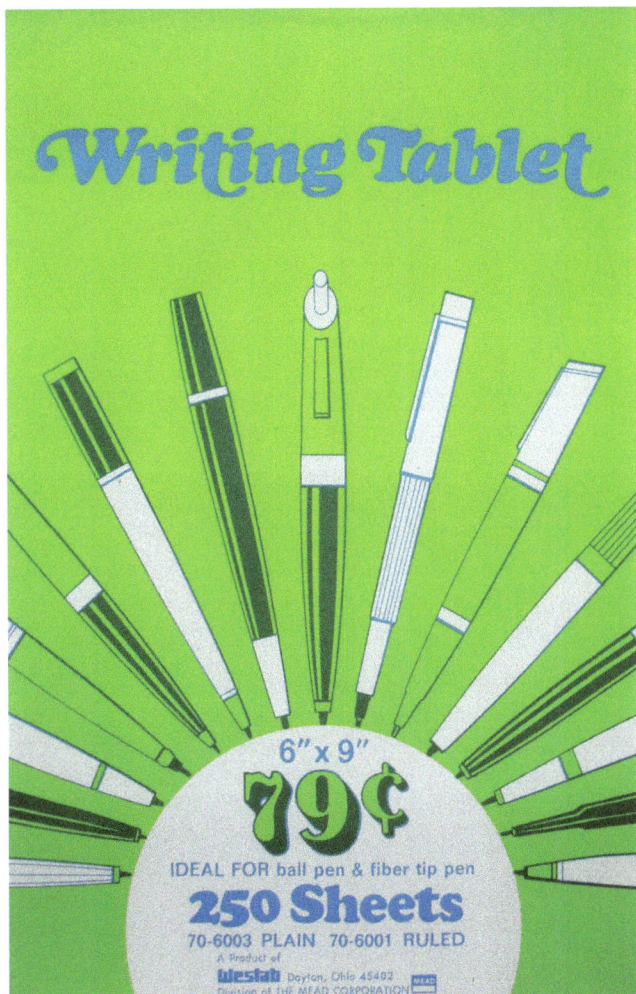

When I got fired, I immediately called him and said I was going on my own, and would he consider to continuing working with me. He agreed, and he'd let me know the next time he had something for me. The only problem was I didn't know how to charge, since I was never involved in the billing process at the agency. He told me not to worry, because each job had a set price, and I would bill him accordingly.

Two months later he called and work rolled in.

For the cover of a new three-ring binder **Westab** was introducing, he told me to "go crazy" and use full color. Up to this point almost all jobs had been two-color.

The binder was a big success, but the inevitable happened. Mead, the parent company of **Westab** changed management, and the both of us lost a job.

The Wet Look logo design I created was for binders that came in glossy vinyl covers. It was also a fashion statement of the time, originating in the UK, where shiny vinyl jackets and trench coats simulating a "wet look" were popular among hip young Mods.

© WESTAB INC.

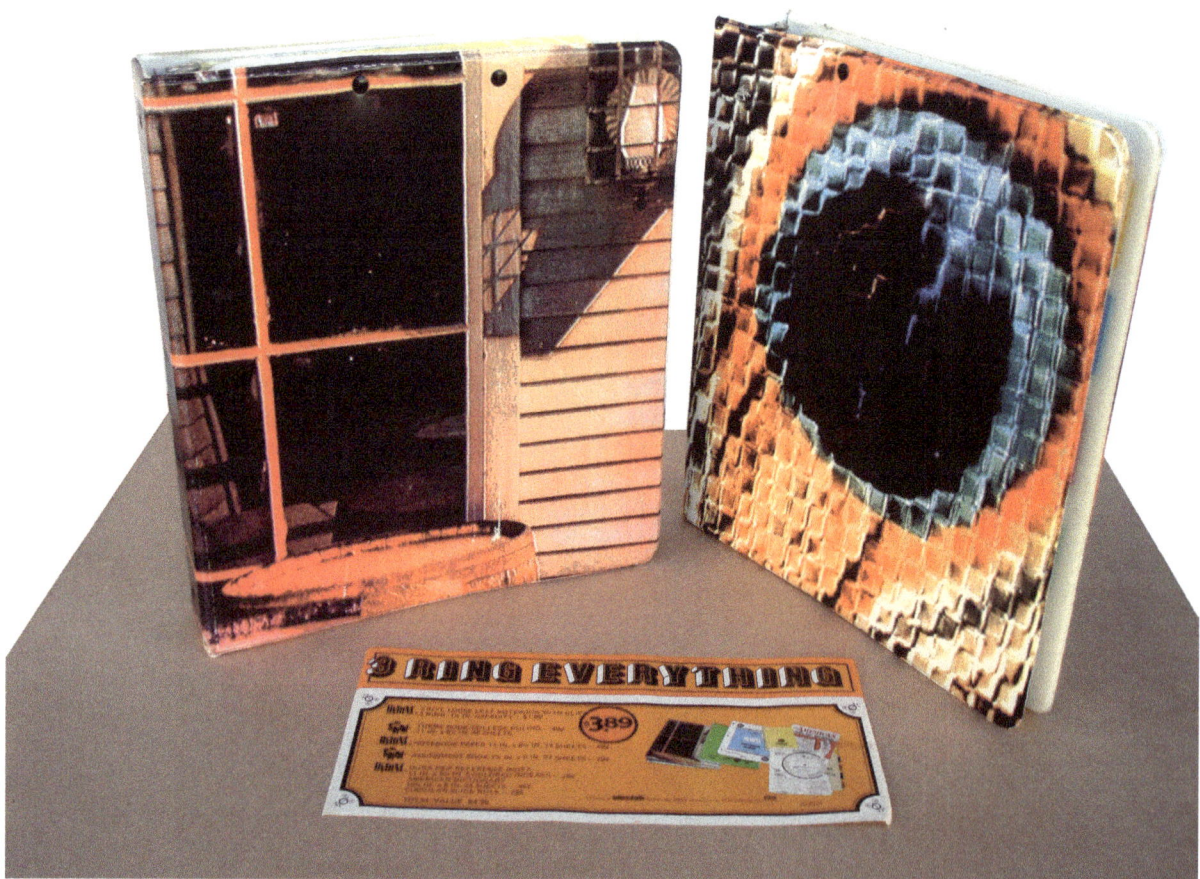

3 RING EVERYTHING

THE CORPORATE IDENTITY PACKAGE

One of the jobs that did not directly involve Steve, was the creation of logos, or corporate identity programs. This was something I really enjoyed, taking a name and representing it graphically so that the logo told the story visually. Some great examples are the CBS logo created in 1951 by William Golden-often referred to as the "eyemark," suggesting that television is an eye on the world.

Another one of my favorites was the Goodwill logo, which is a lowercase "g" that turns into a smiling face, projecting "good-will."

Over the years I created many corporate logos which often led to further work, like brochures, print advertising, and the necessary letterhead, envelope, and business card design to go along with it. In the *Mad Men* series, Don Draper stresses to a subordinate to never present two sample ideas to a client because that shows weakness. Confidently go with one solid idea to present to the potential client. Although the series did not exist at the time we had our agency, it is instinctively what we did. Show one idea and sell the hell out of it, which Steve did with aplomb, doing the talking during our presentation.

Arcadia Savings

The city of Arcadia is known for its free-ranging peacocks, so I inserted the profile of a peacock into the "A" of **Arcadia Savings**. The colors were silver and blue to echo a peacock's colors.

Capistrano Savings

Everyone in Southern California is familiar with the San Juan Capistrano Mission and the annual return of the swallows, which I incorporated into their logo.

Cookin' Wood

I used a chunky type style to suggest the cubed blocks of wood **Cookin' Wood** sold for barbecuing, and to illustrate its function, I set the "i" aflame. The typeface was done in a woodsy brown, with the flame in red.

Redwood Insurance

I placed the image of a giant redwood tree into the negative space of the capital R. The printed colors of the logo were deep red and green

The only time I broke the rule of representing more than one concept was in the presentation of logos. I always did three. My original concept was my favorite, which I'd place in the center of the presentation board, surrounded by two more. About 95% of the time the middle logo was chosen.

The **Redwood Insurance** logo led to a lot of additional work from the company. In one meeting with the president, he was miffed that one of his account executives, in hosting a hotel hospitality suite, had "only spent $6,000" on entertaining potential new customers. Steve and I knew, hearing that, it would be no problem charging our full fees.

In one of our introductory self-promotion brochures, Steve wrote: Logos and corporate graphics are an integral part of our potential service to clients. This "image" is the starting point of communicating to the consumer.

Although running horizontal negative space through a typeface is quite common now, it was pretty innovative when I did it for the **Applied Planning Dynamics** logo, an architectural firm specializing in "engineered planned unit developments."

I was never quite sure what the difference was between a grouping of condos or planned unit developments, but it didn't matter as they loved the logo and brochure we designed.

Leysen/Johnston
ADVERTISING

**CORPORATE IDENTITY IS OUR BUSINESS
CALL US FOR THE SAKE OF YOUR IMAGE**

WE SET THE STAGE

Steve made contact with a small repertory company located streetside in downtown Costa Mesa, founded by David Emmes and Martin Benson. I created a poster for their West Coast Premier of Kurt Vonnegut's play, *Happy Birthday Wanda June*. It was **South Coast Repertory's** first theatrical production of the season and became a smash hit. As Steve said, "We set the stage."

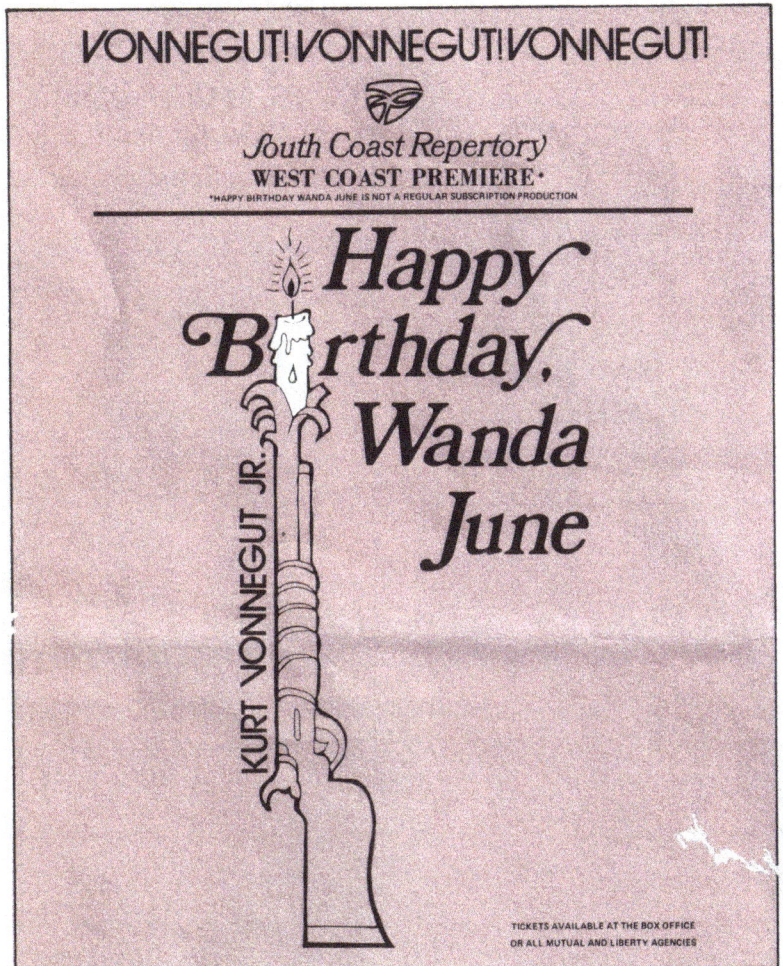

Over the years we would do many promotional items for **SCR**, including the individual theater guides for each successive play. Currently **South Coast Repertory** has grown to national stature with its theater nestled in prime real estate across South Coast Plaza and the nearby Segerstrom Center.

DOING LUNCH

Steve and I made it a habit to go out to lunch everyday and we would "discuss business" as a tax write-off, but at the same time keep an eye out for a potential new client. A restaurant Steve and I frequented, which was within walking distance of our office was **Le Biarritz**. During one lunch, Steve pitched the owner into doing advertising, and he agreed.

I hired Cheryle O'Gara, a photographer, to take photos of the owner and his photogenic wife. I used her in the first and second ad, striking a saucy pose under Steve's headline, "Frankly, we're not expensive." This was to counter the accepted idea that French restaurants were expensive.

Coincidentally, Cheryle was a waitress at **Le Biarritz** who pitched me with her portfolio of photographs, and I hired her on the spot. We would use her for many photo shoots until she moved to Las Vegas and set up her own successful studio photographing mostly high end casino interiors.

For the next ad we did for **Le Biarritz**, I had the owner (who was authentically French) directly look into the camera with a slightly raised hand, as if caught mid-conversation, saying, "It's like coming home…to France."

It's like coming home...to France

Unfortunately, many French restaurants serve a stuffy atmosphere with their fine meals. The delicious experience of French dining is usually left for the well-to-do or the once-in-a-great-while nights out.

That's why we advertise that Le Biarritz is "Hometown France." We still serve superb food, but there are no stuffy waiters, no unreadable menus — no *haute ambiance.*

Join us for award winning dining for lunch or dinner. It's like coming home ...to France.

LE BIARRITZ™
French Restaurant

**Dinner 7 Days. Lunch Monday thru Friday. 414 N. Newport Blvd., Newport Beach.
For Reservations (714) 645-6700. Cocktails.**

BANKING ON IT

One thing about financial institutions, they pay their bills on time. On the surface they may appear conservative, but a new savings and loan would turn out to be quite receptive to our "non-conservative" ideas. **Mariners Savings and Loan**, with their corporate office in Newport Beach had two locations, and during our advertising tenure we helped them grow to seven with TV, radio, direct mail, print, and outdoor advertising. Their circular logo made for a perfectly punned billboard: Steve's brilliant headline:

"The Sum Also Rises."

I showed the logo rising from the horizon upwards to the top of the billboard.

When Mariners still only had two locations, Steve came up with a headline to challenge the larger institutions.

"Bigger isn't Better."

For that I decided to hire Phil Interlandi, a well known cartoonist and *Playboy* regular. He made a terrific cartoon of a man at a tailor getting outfitted in a suit that was obviously two sizes too large. You'll read more about Phil Interlandi later on.

One thing about Newport Beach is that people love the scenic environment they live in. I was commissioned by **Mariners** to do pen and ink drawings of various Newport "landmarks," the locations strictly my choice. These were printed up on large format high- quality paper and given to their customers. Later we formulated these iconic images into a historical booklet called "The Landmark Series", and **Mariners** ended up giving 20,000 copies away.

Western Cannery

A replica of the Cannery occupies the space where this historical landmark once stood. It's located at the entrance to the Lido Peninsula in Cannery Village.

MARK JENSEN

This was the heart of Newport's commercial fishing district. Up to a few years ago, the Western Cannery packed as much as 100 tons of mackerel a day, and as much as 275 million cans of fish a year. It was used mostly as dog and cat food.

Fishing once brought $35 million to this resort's economy. Three canneries were in operation at the peak. Then, water pollution off coastal waters drove the big schools of fish farther and farther out to sea. Commercial fishing soon became economically unfeasable.

The boatyards near the Cannery, once packed with fishing boats like sardines in a can, now offer berth to private boats and restaurant frontage. As a matter of fact, the Western Cannery has been replaced by the Cannery Restaurant. It's a 7/8 exact reproduction of the old fish packing house.

Boat Works

The canals and channels at the north end of Newport Harbor are home to many dry docks and boat works.

MARK LEYSEN

It is a yearly cycle for most boats. Proper maintenance includes hauling, scrubbing, sanding and repainting her bottom. For both private boats and commercial vessels, staying "shipshape" is a constant battle with the sea.

Since the Santa Ana river was diverted in the early 1900's, to make Newport Harbor what it is today, boat repair and maintenance has been a necessary part of the scene. Today, there are 9,000 pleasurecraft registered here and there is a waiting list six years long for precious moorings and slips.

The harbor contains seven islands. Some, like Balboa Island, were artificially built by dredging silt from the murky bay bottom. Property on these islands and the surrounding waterfront is understandably high priced, with mid-six figure ranges not uncommon. Many of the boat works have given up their space for restaurants and private dwellings.

CIAO ALFA

Through a connection with a local car dealership, we set up a meeting with Southern California's marketing director of **Alfa Romeo**. When we met with him in his sleek corporate office, he showed off a fancy coffee machine. He poured us two cups, which became our first cappuccinos.

"Do you know where the name cappuccini comes from?" he asked.

We had no idea.

"From the capuchin monkey. White hair on top, with a brown body underneath, just like your coffee - white on top brown underneath."

A new term had then popped up in advertising called "positioning." **Alfa** was competing with Porsche, and Steve came up with a terrific headline.

**MY ALFA ROMEO
PUTS A 924 PORSCHE OUT OF THE PICTURE.**

Now I had to find a way to "position" the **Alfa Romeo** against the Porsche. We hired a model, had her dress in a short skirted tennis outfit (very Newport), and placed her atop the Alfa. I asked her to smile, kick one leg up, and the photo was taken.

Our advertising sold lots of **Alfa Romeos**, so many in fact that the marketing director switched to a larger advertising agency. Their success was our loss. *Arrivederci Alfa!*

WHAT IS IT?

Occasionally a client came to us with a product we had no idea what it was. And one of those was **WEI Corporation** that produced heat sinks. In our initial meeting with the client we quickly learned how the product functioned, and as Steve wrote:

What's a heat sink? Ask any electrical engineer and he'll say he couldn't work without one. They make it cool when things get hot. Next time you're into the back end of a computer (which were pretty large back then), *look for the funny metal butterflies, that's a kind of heat sink.*

I took a straight-on photo of a heat sink (made out of extruded aluminum) and duplicated it to cover the front of their brochure I designed. The **WEI** logo was also a simplified graphic representation of a heat sink.

Although we had a fairly good idea what a truss was, in this case it was a company that manufactured them strictly for housing development. We picked up **Kimtruss** as a client, and their first request was a logo.

This led to us doing a full color catalog, and I also designed graphics for the cabs of their semis. In our promotion brochure Steve wrote:

Kimtruss helps put roofs over a lot of people's heads.

They make prefabricated trusses for the building industry.

In a way, our advertising helps support a "supporting" industry.

Unfortunately, **Kimtruss** was bought out by a large Australian conglomerate, and we lost them as a client. The saying in the ad business is: Pretty much any client you have, you will lose somewhere down the road. It could be a change in a company's marketing director's position, or a buy-out by a larger company, or they grew to a point where they want a bigger agency.

For over 30 years the choice has been Kimtruss

Kimtruss is the number one building [truss] manufacturer in the West. For three decades more architects, [engin]eers and builders have specified [t]russes by name.

[Th]e reason is simple: **Consistent** [Qua]**lity, Complete Engineering** [Assi]**stance** and **Proven Economy.** [Whe]n it comes to building trusses— [the] word is Kimtruss.

Your success is our business

Every project is a challenge. From simple **commercial construction** to **complex designs** into the thousands of units, we supply the engineering expertise to meet or exceed project demands.

We work as a team with our clients and follow each job to its successful completion…on time, on budget!

THE ORIGIN STORY

One thing about choosing a partner is that you need to be compatible, which is not to say we didn't have minor disagreements, but it was all in the pursuit of creating a better ad or campaign. The joke among our peers was that our eighteen-year partnership lasted longer than most Orange County marriages.

Steve Johnston   *Mark Leysen*

I first met Steve in our high school junior year. He lived a clamshell's throw away from the beach. We started body surfing together, and years later at our ad agency during the times the waves were running, we'd turn our lunch hour into body surfing sessions — a real perk when you're your own boss. Our offices were never farther away from the beach than two-to-three miles, and we even had an in-office shower.

We double-dated, and one of those dates would later become my wife. And to put that into perspective, regarding Orange County marriage statistics, we are still married.

During the occasional down time while in between clients, Steve and I would sit around trying to come up with an idea to produce something that had nothing to with our advertising. After bouncing around a lot of off-the-wall ideas, none of which I can now recall (possibly marijuana was involved), we settled on a concept, which would be a slim funny paperback, Steve titled *The Newport Beach Answer Book*. This was meant to poke mild fun at Newport society's affluent upper class.

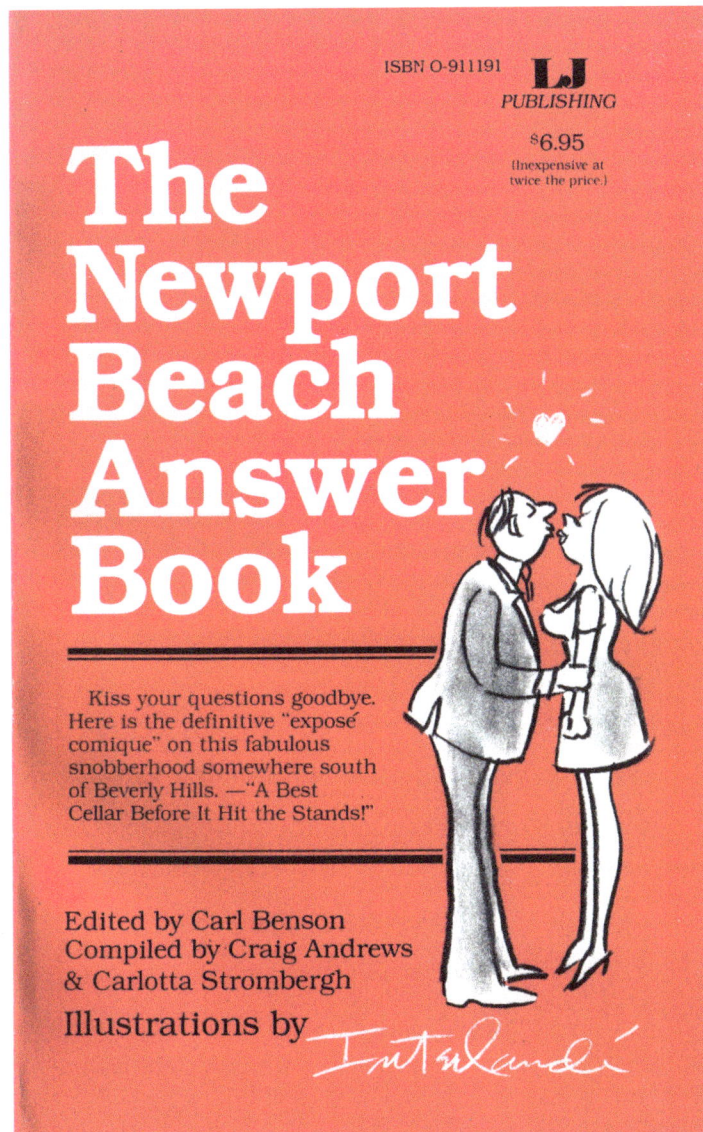

ISBN 0-911191

LJ
PUBLISHING

$6.95
(Inexpensive at twice the price.)

The Newport Beach Answer Book

Kiss your questions goodbye. Here is the definitive "exposé comique" on this fabulous snobberhood somewhere south of Beverly Hills. —"A Best Cellar Before It Hit the Stands!"

Edited by Carl Benson
Compiled by Craig Andrews
& Carlotta Strombergh
Illustrations by *Interlandi*

Once more, I turned to Phil Interlandi to do the illustrations, except this time his fee would be out-of-pocket for us, since it was our independent project, without a client footing the bill. Phil had been a one time art director at a prominent Chicago advertising agency, but moved west to Laguna Beach to "live a semi-retired life in freelance cartoonery." Besides *Playboy* as a main client, Phil went on to illustrate Art Linkletter's book, "I Wish I'd Said That,"and Ed MacMahon's "Barside Companion."

I was looking to get about a dozen or so black and white drawings out of him and feared his fee might be too much. I set up a meeting with Phil to get together at the Ivy House in Laguna Beach, a hangout for several other *Playboy* cartoonists as well. Phil's brother, Frank, did an OpEd panel in the LA Times under the shadow of Paul Conrad, Pulitzer prize winning cartoonist who always got a bigger placement.

When I walked into the backroom of the Ivy House I could hear rowdy laughter and the loud banter of jokes- many inappropriate by today's standards, as I suppose a few of our *The Newport Beach Answer Book* pages were also. Times change.

Stepping up to the bar, the first thing Phil asked was, "What kind of stiff drink can I get you?"

It was three in the afternoon, and I politely declined.

He stared at me. "What? You can't say you're in advertising if you don't drink!"

This was made pretty clear in the *Mad Men* TV series, as the main characters seem to drink (the hard stuff) around the clock. I got a beer.

I pitched Phil our concept which he went for, and told him how many drawings I needed, and he gave me his estimate, which was way beyond our budget. I tried not to spill my beer. I explained that all the jokes were already written; he just had to illustrate them.

"Oh, you mean I don't have to come with any of the taglines? Cool."

He considerably lowered his price, and I left him with a typed copy of the finished jokes Steve and I had put together.

For the cover I chose a "hot pink", which I figured would have eye-catching shelf appeal. We printed 5000 copies, and they quickly sold out.

Newport Beach Women are really terrific housekeepers!

In every divorce settlement they keep the house!

How does a Newport Beach Man get turned on by his wife?

She pretends she's his tennis partner.

What's a memorable vacation for a Newport Beach Couple?

Separate.

What kind of secretary does a Newport Beach Executive like to hire?

One that comes through in a pinch.

According to one bookstore, the president of a bronze plating company bought 50 copies, one each for his employees as a Christmas gift. At a slim 64 pages, we priced the book at the then outrageous price of $6.95. We printed another 1000 copies and sold those out also. *The Orange County Register* wrote an article about the book and asked if we were ready to expand and do an "The LA Answer Book," or "The San Francisco Answer Book," but we really had no inside scoop on those cities, nor had the desire to do the research.

I was interviewed by the *LA Times*, and photographed in one of the bookstores holding the book, which made for more sales. *The Times* asked, *"Can Newport Take a Joke?"*

Some of our friends wondered if we were biting the hand that fed us in our satirical commentary and "adult" situations regarding Newport Beach. I suppose if we'd belonged to the John Wayne Tennis Club, they might have revoked our membership.

Steve and I were big fans of our newly elected California Governor, Jerry Brown, who would go on to be elected governor for an astounding four times. What we liked about him was that he embraced a kind of Zen philosophy ideology, making quotes that one didn't expect from a politician.

Steve started collecting Brown's one or two-liner aphorisms that appeared in the newspapers, and handed them to me to illustrate. This time, I took on various styles for his quotes to make it look like the book had been illustrated by several artists.

We called the book **Jerry Brown Verbatim**.

Big problem: It seemed a lot of people didn't know what "verbatim" meant. The book was pretty much a flop and didn't sell well, and I take partial blame for that. The cover I designed was a high contrast extreme close-up of Brown's face… unlike the glowing hot pink cover for the "Newport Beach Answer Book," it lacked as they say – shelf appeal.

We did get newspaper coverage with a large photo of Steve and I holding the book, but it didn't help. We mailed a complimentary copy to Jerry Brown, who thanked us but sent it back, "I don't accept gifts," he wrote. That put an end to our self-publishing venture.

Yet, rather mysteriously copies of our slim Jerry Brown Verbatim can now be bought on ebay for a rather pricey $40.

Perhaps there's some kind of nostalgic following for JBV after all these years.

KISS

In today's times, a person will be exposed to more images in a twenty-four hour period than someone would see in a whole lifetime back in 1900. That's a lot of clutter. The idea that can work well 90% of the time is KISS, or Keep It Simple Stupid. What that pretty much means is creating a headline with seven words or less, as Bernbach so succinctly pointed out in his early VW ads. An example was Steve's headline for a redwood hot tub account.

Obviously not every ad headline could be resolved in seven words or less, but we felt that shorter was better.

Steve and I had landed the **Sequoia Hot Tub** account and I was looking for a model to pose in one of their tubs. On lunch one day at the Red Onion, in the heart of Newport Beach facing the bay, we were served by a tall (six foot one) blonde, lithesome waitress with a killer smile.

I asked, "How would you like to be in an advertisement?"

She gave me the look and in a strong Australian accent said,"Mate, that's what they all say."

She assumed it was a pickup line, and I assured her I was serious. I gave her my business card: Mark Leysen, Art Director, Leysen/Johnston Advertising. Steve quickly gave her his card that yes indeed he was the Johnston in Leysen/Johnston.

I can't remember what minimum pay for a waitress was back then, but when I offered her $60 per hour for a three hour shoot, she said, "I'll be there." Then she turned and asked, "What should I wear?"

"Little as possible," I replied.

As luck would have it she also brought along a very presentable girl-friend who didn't charge for the cou-ples in the tub shot, where Steve and I decided to "hire ourselves" as the male models. Her friend was paid in free wine, and happy for the simple plea-sure of seeing herself in an ad. Ah, the allure of print advertising.

WE WANT TO GET YOU INTO HOT WATER!

Sequoia Spa needs a few selected dealers for an expanding and highly profitable market in Redwood Hot Tubs. We are a manufacturing company with a proven sales record.

Our selected dealer programs provide a complete package of training, quality Hot Tubs and accessories, complete sales brochures and advertising materials for media. You'll have everything you need to get into Hot Water...a very profitable business!

There are several types of dealer programs to choose from. If you're a potential dealer, contact the company with experience and quality. We have installed more Redwood Hot Tubs than anyone else! Call Sequoia Spa today. (714) 957-8992.

Or write: **Mr. Ralph Benware, Sequoia Spa, 1805 E. Dyer Road, Santa Ana, Cal. 92705**

SEQUOIA S SPA

1145 E. Dominguez St., Carson
(213) 639-1621 • Factory and Showroom

1805 E. Dyer Road, Santa Ana
(714) 957-8992 • Showroom and Factory

ONE NIGHT STAND

There were times when a client approached us requiring only one thing: a brochure to highlight their services. Once that was completed, they had no further use for us. One such client was **Acra-Cast Foundries, Inc**, located in Compton. They produced a host of non-ferrous metal castings that included everything from fire hydrants, locks and latches, to shipboard pumps and valves.

While Steve was taking copious notes interviewing the owner, I was cut loose in the 30,000 square ft. facility with Cheryle O'Gara, our photographer, who I instructed to shoot at will. Later, I would assemble the photos I thought best, plus Steve's comprehensive body copy into a slick two-color brochure with a dynamic cover.

ACRA-CAST
FOUNDRIES, INC.

VOICE OVER

FREEDOMS
FOUNDATION
at VALLEY FORGE

One of our strengths as an agency was Steve's voice. While he was in the army stationed in Germany at Armed Forces Network, he wrote, produced and voiced radio ads and plays, winning the Thomas Jefferson Freedom Award for a dramatic production on soldiers going into battle in World War I.

As we started to offer radio spots to our clients, Steve with his experience as both producer and radio DJ filled the role perfectly, which meant we didn't have to hire outside talent, saving us a bundle in voice-over costs. Steve could do serious, funny, and anything in between voices for whatever the product or service required.

Some of his voice work for clients included **Air Canada**, **Wild West Stores**, and **Squibb**, a large pharmaceutical company.

Steve connected with a Christian publisher who commissioned him to do a dramatization of the Bible, word for word to be recorded on tape — this being the pre CD era. Almost everyone had a cassette recorder either at home or in their car. People might not have the patience to read the Bible, but they would listen to it. In studio, it took Steve nine months of recording time, plus hiring several leading actors from **South Coast Repertory** to voice various Biblical characters to complete the project. Over time, 100,000,000 cassettes, CDs, MP3s, and DVDs were sold.

NETWORKING

At Steve's church he was introduced to the owner of **Van Dell and Associates**, a civil engineering firm.

The thing to remember is that you need to be ready to sell yourself to the next client, and if it's church, so be it.

Although Steve and I were not big fans of wining and dining a client, we did invite the owner out to lunch to pitch what kind of work we could do for him. He ordered a steak, which he copiously covered with butter. When he ran out, I offered him mine. Anyway, we landed the account which called for two separate corporate brochures plus a logo. You could say we buttered him up.

Below: Inside spread Van Dell Associates brochure.

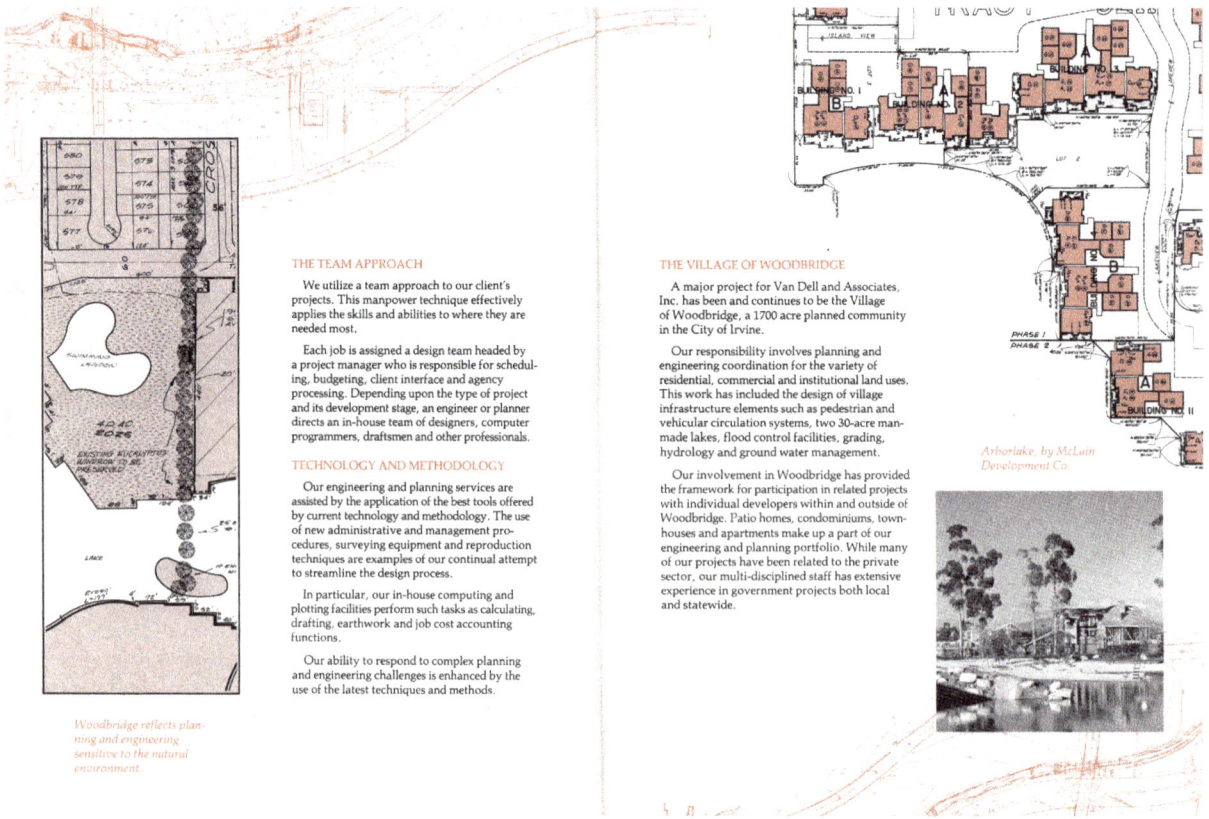

THE TEAM APPROACH

We utilize a team approach to our client's projects. This manpower technique effectively applies the skills and abilities to where they are needed most.

Each job is assigned a design team headed by a project manager who is responsible for scheduling, budgeting, client interface and agency processing. Depending upon the type of project and its development stage, an engineer or planner directs an in-house team of designers, computer programmers, draftsmen and other professionals.

TECHNOLOGY AND METHODOLOGY

Our engineering and planning services are assisted by the application of the best tools offered by current technology and methodology. The use of new administrative and management procedures, surveying equipment and reproduction techniques are examples of our continual attempt to streamline the design process.

In particular, our in-house computing and plotting facilities perform such tasks as calculating, drafting, earthwork and job cost accounting functions.

Our ability to respond to complex planning and engineering challenges is enhanced by the use of the latest techniques and methods.

Woodbridge reflects planning and engineering sensitive to the natural environment.

THE VILLAGE OF WOODBRIDGE

A major project for Van Dell and Associates, Inc. has been and continues to be the Village of Woodbridge, a 1700 acre planned community in the City of Irvine.

Our responsibility involves planning and engineering coordination for the variety of residential, commercial and institutional land uses. This work has included the design of village infrastructure elements such as pedestrian and vehicular circulation systems, two 30-acre man-made lakes, flood control facilities, grading, hydrology and ground water management.

Our involvement in Woodbridge has provided the framework for participation in related projects with individual developers within and outside of Woodbridge. Patio homes, condominiums, townhouses and apartments make up a part of our engineering and planning portfolio. While many of our projects have been related to the private sector, our multi-disciplined staff has extensive experience in government projects both local and statewide.

Arborlake, by McLain Development Co.

Steve also made another connection at his church with the principal of a certified public accounting firm, which I designed a corporate identity program for. Ironically, in their reception area, they had a pew for their waiting clientele.

The marketing director at **Mariners Savings and Loan** was a member of the **Balboa Bay Club**. He introduced us to the president of the **BBC** (as it was often referred to) who was looking to produce a full-color brochure on the club's amenities and services.

Although neither Steve nor I could afford to buy a **BBC** membership we did get a free lunch.

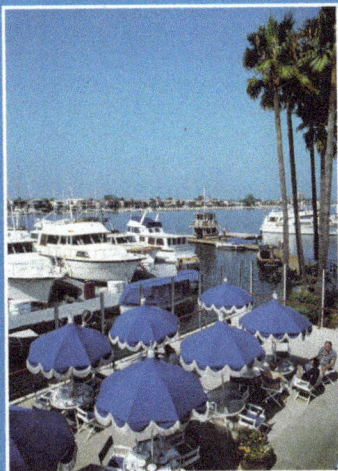

One of the few private waterfront clubs in the United States…A landmark since 1948.

A LUXURY HOME AWAY FROM HOME
The Balboa Bay Club is a tradition filled with pleasure, recreation and convenience. For a family getaway, corporate business or private meetings the BBC offers a not-for-everyone waterfront club.

Fine dining, a private beach, sophisticated in-club recreation, waterfront and view guestrooms, spas, personal fitness consultation. It's all a part of the BBC. Your world apart.

THE CORPORATE WORLD
For your business, we offer everything any hotel or convention center offers, except we are not a hotel or convention center. Our 14 meeting rooms include complete audio-visual support and individual design for reception, schoolroom, conference or theater.
Your business meetings can take place intimately with waterfront dining or in our largest conference room. They will always be a breath of fresh air.

MEMBERSHIP WITH A VIEW
Single, family or corporate membership in the Balboa Bay Club is the best Newport Beach has to offer. There are scheduled events for children and adults. Plus, supervised recreation and programs designed for education. Membership is an investment in pleasure and privacy. It's just knowing that you have a private place to be at ease in elegance.

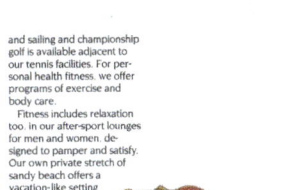

IN-CLUB FITNESS AND RECREATION
Our in-club facilities offer tennis, racquetball, squash, a complete spa for men and women, two large swimming pools, gymnasium, boating and sailing and championship golf is available adjacent to our tennis facilities. For personal health fitness, we offer programs of exercise and body care.
Fitness includes relaxation too, in our after-sport lounges for men and women, designed to pamper and satisfy. Our own private stretch of sandy beach offers a vacation-like setting for maximizing that healthy look.

HOW BIG SHOULD A CLIENT BE?

A truism in advertising is:

Never have a client who is more than 60% of your business.

Because if they leave, you're left pretty high and dry. We stuck to that formula as best we could, and when **Mariners Savings and Loan** merged with a larger financial institution, we lost a big account but certainly not 60%, more like 35% which hurt, but it wasn't devastating.

We scrambled for new clients to fill the gap, and I for one pitched a new sleek furniture store and got the account. It was a nice relationship that was exclusively newspaper ad based and lasted for a short two years when the owner decided he wanted to open a French bakery instead in Laguna Beach, closing his furniture store. His bakery was located street side on the Coast Highway with plenty of drive-by and pedestrian visibility. His bakery didn't require any advertising. C'est la vie.

Occasionally we got lucky and a client walked in ready to hand us work without needing a pitch. One such client was **West Coast Helicopter**. I designed their logo, business card, envelope and letterhead, plus created a small brochure that offered their services. One of West Coast's unusual features was that they flew the helicopters for the hit TV show, M.A.S.H.

As Steve wrote: "We helped them get off the ground."

Every time I watched M.A.S.H, I would think, "Hey, my logo is on the side the camera doesn't show."

Another walk-in was **Real Manufacturing** which produced a line of California Bath Products. I designed labels for a whole array of scented bath essentials and vitamin E

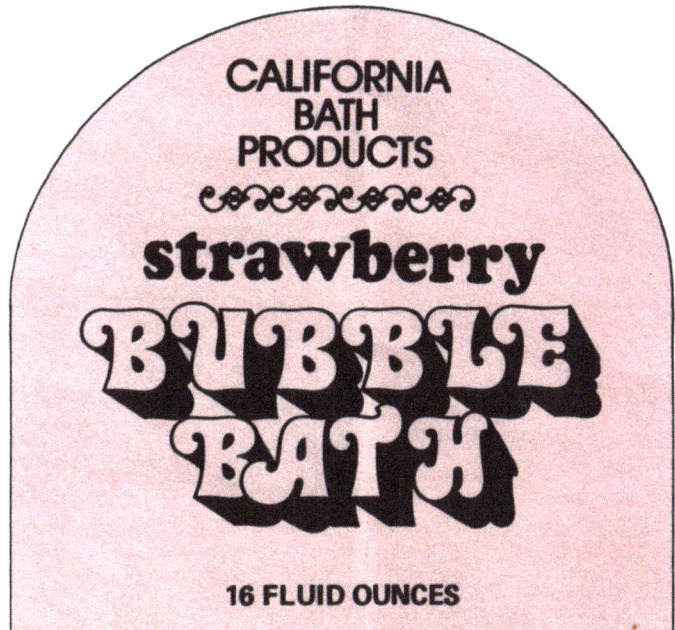

tanning cream. Their line was sold in boutiques, head shops, and drug stores. I personally liked their strawberry shampoo, and you could say we kept it "Real."

With some of our new clients we were able to fill in the void that **Mariners Saving and Loan** left us with.

Although I never got into SUP (Stand Up Paddling), we did get a walk-in client one day that was ready to open a store selling kayaks, paddle boards, and various SUP products. She needed a logo that could be applied to decals, banners, sales tags, and the front window of her retail store on the Balboa Peninsula. I came up with a design of a paddle that straddled a diamond shape, the top part above **Paddle Power** suggesting a pyramid, sometimes referred to as a symbol of strength or power.

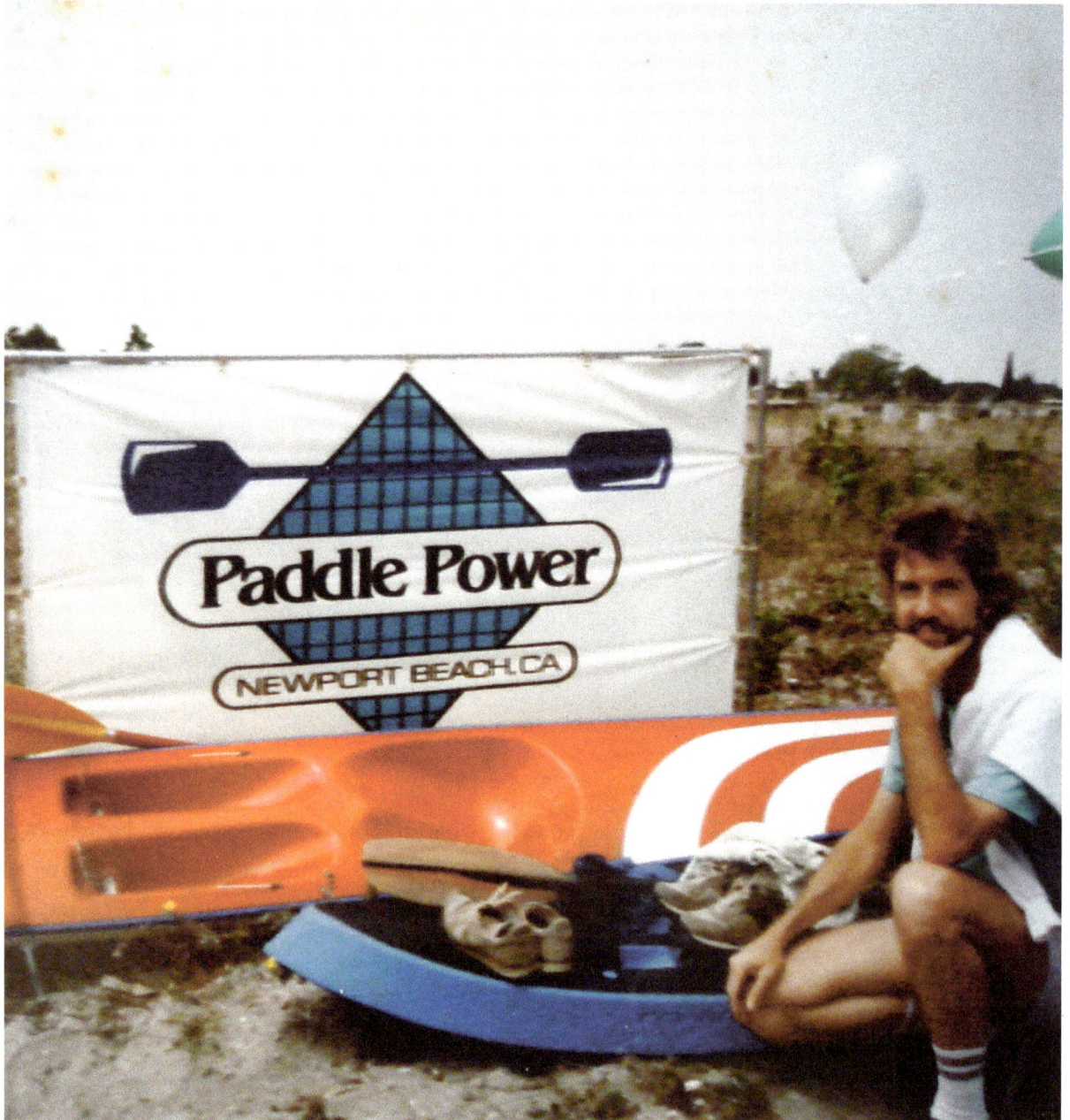

In the 70's and 80's Orange County's real estate market started booming. We knew of one agency that devoted about 90% of its ad revenues to real estate projects. To me this seemed like sheer boredom to come to work every day and tout another subdivision development. However we did land several developers on our own, one being **Marina Pacifica,** a huge condominium complex at the Long Beach Marina. Their marketing director was a transplanted New Yorker named Norm Danoff, who at one time worked for Doyle Dane Bernbach.

Bill Bernbach created the show stopping VW ad that simply said "**Lemon**" in bold sans serif type. Reading the body copy, it pointed out that a mere scratch on the chrome around the glove compartment would get the car taken off the delivery line. Or as it was succinctly pointed out, "We pluck the lemons, you get the plums."

The **Marina Pacifica** homes had terrific views of the expansive bay (years later used for Olympic rowing competitions), and our first print ad carried Steve's headline above a photo of a sumptuous living room interior with high ceilings and windows, that stated boldly:

You can be one of the chosen view.

It wasn't a seven-word headline at eight, but was close. Norm handed us tons of work that included radio spots, print ads, and complex multi-page brochures. Norm's executive secretary later went out on her own and handed us **Warner Electric**, a client that was involved in the development of shopping centers and hospitals who needed a full-color brochure. The brochure was a big hit, save for one minor detail, buried in the body copy; we'd spelled the word "licence" the British way instead of "license", the standard American English way. Well, no one is perfect.

Lemon.

You can be one of the chosen view.

If you really want to live when you retire, live at Marina Pacifica! We offer you security and convenience, plus a waterfront home that makes you one of the chosen view.

Every one of our maintenance free condominiums overlooks the water, with boatslips immediately available to homeowners.

You enter Marina Pacifica through a Security Gate, then park your car underground, away from the weather. A quick elevator ride takes you to your one, two or three bedroom home. Inside is the warmth of plush carpeting, broad beam ceilings and unique amenities found nowhere else.

You can retire with the "chosen view". We're snuggled privately on the Long Beach Marina.

DIRECTIONS: From the San Diego Freeway, take the Studebaker Road Turn-off and follow the signs south to Second Street, then right to Marina Pacifica.

1, 2, 3 bedroom Waterfront Condominiums from **$50,000** to **$125,000**

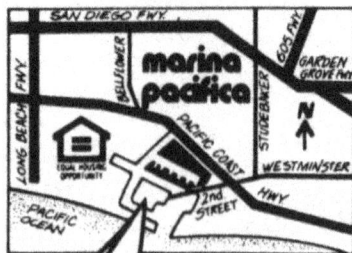

6201 East 2nd Street, Long Beach • Phone (213) 430-0574
Furnished Models Open .m. to Dusk

marina pacifica
AT THE LONG BEACH MARINA

48

WARNER ELECTRIC INC.

Torrance Hospital
Torrance, California
Warner Electric completed two major
additions to this hospital complex.

East L. A. Comprehensive Health Center
Los Angeles, California

V. A. Hospital
Long Beach, California
Warner Electric completed a major addition and
installed the new main service and feeders.
Similar installations are also being done by
Warner at the Sepulveda and Wadsworth
V. A. facilities.

J. C. Penney
Fox Hills Mall
Culver City, California

Petrolane
Long Beach, California

49

Even with the "licence" misuse, she referred us to one more large electrical company. Like **Warner**, **KIRKWOOD Electric** was also involved in huge building projects including doing the electrical for Disney's "America Sings" exhibit.

SYSTEMS

*Computer based
animation control*

From Disneyland's "America Sings"
exhibit to Kerr-McGee's automated
mining process and material handling
installation, Kirkwood's experience
spans the spectrum of electrical control
and power utilization systems.
Kirkwood management and technical
skills are combined to prepare the most
sophisticated modern-day systems for
on-time startup. Our total concept
approach is guaranteed
to get the job done.

CHOOSING A CITY

In real estate, it's often about location, location, location. As we enlarged our offices and moved to different locations we always made sure we had a Newport Beach address. It gave us the perception of success.

One of our clients, a developer, had recently finished an apartment complex that was a short hop away from the Newport Beach border. In our ads we included the street address, contact phone, but he did not want to have it in print that his development was located in Costa Mesa, so we omitted it from the ads. Instead Steve wrote, "Only blocks away from the scenic Newport Back Bay."

Later Nike would get caught flatfooted when they opened a multi-story retail space in Triangle Square, right in the heart of Costa Mesa. The address was on Newport Boulevard, and they incorrectly added Newport Beach in all their advertising. Nike was eventually told to remove Newport Beach as the city, but they never added Costa Mesa, giving potential customers the perception that surely Newport Boulevard was indeed in Newport Beach, which always seems to carry more cachet.

The nice thing about working with developers was that they supplied the art. Architectural firms made renderings of what the project would look like before it was even built, and we incorporated those drawings into our ads and brochures I designed.

Right: Nantucket Condominium Development

DRESS FOR SUCCESS

Moving into the 80's, people started to get more casual about what they wore, and since we were called "creatives", no one expected us to dress like Wall Street brokers. We let our hair get longer, grew short trimmed beards and got into denims. One morning getting ready to pitch a new potential financial account in downtown Long Beach, we happened to show up at the office in almost identical jeans and denim jackets. Their headquarters was in a slick highrise building, and when we approached the financial marketing director, she took one look at us, and I knew things would not go well. She cut the meeting short by saying that she had an "emergency meeting" to attend and would call us. It never happened. Evidently we had projected just too much denim.

If we'd been pitching Miller's Outpost, a hip clothing store, things might have gone better. However a year or so later Steve signed them up to do radio spots. And at Millers I bought a suede leather jacket with fringe. I was no Easy Rider, but it was cool to pretend.

INSPIRATION

Ideas can come from literally anywhere - while in the shower, driving on the freeway, or getting ready to nod off in bed. In that semi-subconscious state, when all other noise and chatter is removed, ideas often filter in. I always kept a notepad on my nightstand in case an idea hit me so I could write it down.

There's a famous scene in *Mad Men* where one of the main characters is in his office knocking back a few stiff ones, pondering an idea for a campaign. Finally he says, "I've got it," and then falls asleep on his couch. Later when he's asked if he's come up with anything, "He says, yeah… but I didn't write it down."

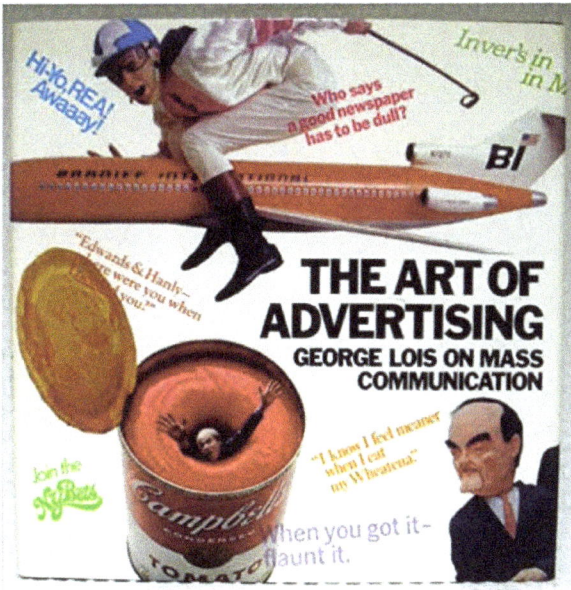

If you're drawing a blank, one way to get inspired is to look at ads done by other agencies. Let's face it, everyone does it. In 1977 I bought the oversized glossy hardback, *The Art of Advertising* by George Lois. He was a New York ad man, and one of my idols who pretty much pioneered the copywriter/art director combo approach and did away with the former practice of using a committee to create an ad. His book was on a shelf behind me, and occasionally it became a terrific reference for spurring a graphic idea.

Two other inspirational greats in the graphic art field are the outstanding designers, Paul Rand and Saul Bass. Rand created the IBM logo plus all their corporate packaging among many other noteworthy designs. Bass produced the iconic movie posters for *Man With the Golden Arm*, and *Vertigo*. Look them up.

However, brainstorming and kicking ideas around, and staying loose is the best way to start the creative process. No matter how outlandish ideas might seem at first, eventually they get whittled down to the essential concept, and the work begins. It's all about keeping an open mind. Another cliche of the times was, *"Like a parachute, the mind works best when it's open."*

SELF PROMOTION

Sooner or later, an agency will have to create an ad to promote itself. We decided to celebrate our 7th year in business by taking out an ad in a glossy monthly magazine describing our services. Our current clients congratulated us, and we picked up one new one. It was a client neither of us ever expected to get, a dentist. He was located in Utah, and just happened to buy the magazine at the John Wayne airport. He saw the ad, and called us for a meeting, driving to our office to introduce himself.

Besides his regular dental practice, he owned a dental lab called **Arrowhead International**, and also toured the country giving lectures to dentists on the principles of practice management. I designed the Arrowhead logo to suggest the letter A with an internal arrowhead.

For each upcoming event we designed ads for dental journals, and direct mail pieces elaborating the benefits of attending his paid seminars. I created a series of slides to highlight his lectures, in effect doing PowerPoint before the term came into usage.

Las Vegas, Hawaii, Newport Beach, and even Bergen, Norway were some of his venues. I had to make several trans-Atlantic phone calls to Thor, the Norwegian seminar contact, who always seemed like he was on his third drink. But it all worked out. We were never very clear why the doctor had chosen Bergen, other than maybe it had a university recognized for its world-renowned museum collection, and it has the country's deepest and longest fjord.

Right: Inside spread Arrowhead Management Systems International brochure.

THE PROS AND CONS OF COMPUTER MANAGEMENT

COMPUTERS AND YOUR PRACTICE

We, as healthcare professionals, cannot ignore the potential of computers in practice management. They reduce the time it takes to perform repetitive administrative tasks and free you and your staff to perform more productive functions.

According to a recent survey of healthcare practices, most practitioners spend eight hours of their 40-hour week on non-patient care activities. A computer can make those eight hours more productive.

DO YOU NEED A COMPUTER?

You can expect direct financial payoffs in using a computer. Staff workload will be reduced. Cash flow will be enhanced by using the computer in collections, and by easing frequent billing of insurance. In the future, processing of insurance claim forms through direct telephone computer hook-up will offer vast savings.

If you have questions about how a computer might or might not benefit your practice, it's best to call on an expert.

Toll Free 1-800-854-4793
In Alaska, Hawaii, California
Call Collect (714) 875-0491

Arrowhead has on-staff experts who can analyze whether or not you should invest. Our experts show you the cost versus the benefit of computerizing any practice management applications. They will develop clear, detailed objectives pertaining to your needs. These objectives will help you make educated decisions for your own computer system comparison.

The doctor invited Steve and I to meet with him in Salt Lake City to introduce us to his staff, which included his dental lab partner, two executive secretaries, and one assistant. We met in an upscale restaurant and were seated at a round table. For some reason the waitress approached me first and asked what I'd like to drink, and I replied "beer."

Immediately I was hit with a cumulative stony glare from the doctor and his associates. It dawned on me that Salt Lake City was Mormon country, so I said, "I'll have coffee instead."

That was no better, since caffeine and alcohol are all verboten by the Mormons. "How about Sanka?" I pleaded.

When I looked around the restaurant I noticed that iced tea evidently was the golden standard for the lunch crowd. Fortunately my drink faux pas didn't lose the account.

The meeting resulted in us picking up a brochure he needed delineating his consulting service (the logo was gold embossed on the glossy cover). One of the inside subheads - which now seems so outdated- asked dentists the big question: "DO YOU NEED A COMPUTER?"

However, he did come up with a catch phrase that Steve and I emulated, which was: Work smarter not harder.

Our relationship with the dentist was long and productive, ending when he retired.

Another way to self-promote is to throw an office party, which means we went through a lot of booze and hors d'oeuvres. I don't know if it ever netted us any new clients, but it was a treat to mix it up informally with the marketing directors and principals of their respective businesses while tying one on.

Right: Commemorative T-shirt design for our 7th Anniversary office party and giveaway promo item.

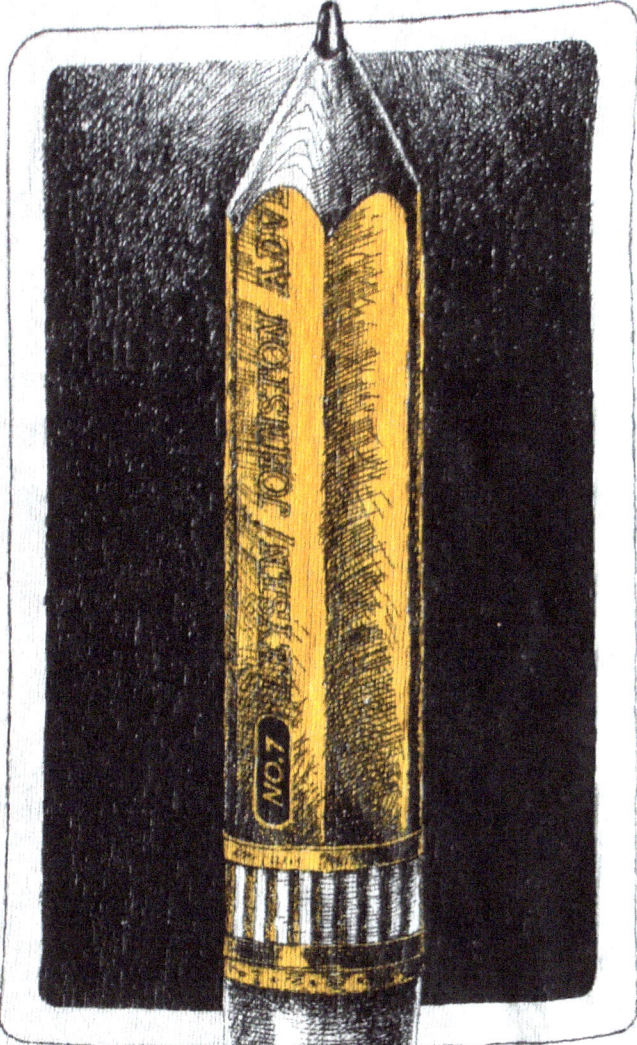

Leysen/Johnston

PARTY FINISHER 1979

7th YEAR

REJECTING A CLIENT

Steve and I used to kid around that if we were approached by a cigarette company, we'd reject them because we were both avid non-smokers. Of course the possibility of Big Tobacco hiring us would be about one in a million. They were BIG and we were SMALL.

However we did have one potential client we had some reservations about. He was running for an unaffiliated city council position, where neither Republican nor Democrat was identified on the ballot. Even though we disagreed with a few ideas of his platform, his opposition was not anyone we'd support. He had a limited budget that called for the design of a bumper sticker and print ads in the local paper.

He lost.

It was our only venture into political campaining.

David Ogilvy of the world renown ad agency Ogilvy & Mather wrote: *"When the client bullies the agency to such an extent that the morale of staff is seriously impaired and starts hurting their performance…It's time to resign the account."*

Fortunately, Steve and I never had to tend with a bullying client, and generally it was smooth sailing.

WHAT'S IT WORTH?

The existential question in advertising always has been: What's an idea worth? And as mentioned previously, an idea can come to you just as easily while driving on the freeway, taking a shower, or while sitting at your desk. After you make that presentation to a new client their first response is going to be: How much will it cost? They have no clue as to how much time you put into creating their ad, logo, or brochure. Could be one hour or one week.

When you quote your price, one of two things will happen: 1. The client readily pulls out their checkbook which means you could have charged more. 2. The client balks and says something to the effect, "It's more than we anticipated." At this point never bid against yourself. Let the client carry the ball by asking, "How much did you expect to pay for this?" They'll offer a lower sum, and if it's agreeable, you shake hands. If it's too low, you can respond by saying, "Actually to make this really look great, we'll need a bit more." Generally the client will up his initial sum somewhat, and a compromise is made.

WHAT IS A BOUTIQUE AGENCY?

In general terms it is a small operation, often a two-person partnership not bogged down by committees, countless vice presidents, or stockholders more interested in bottom line profits rather than producing great advertising.

A client walking through the door would be assured of one thing; and that is they'd be able to deal with the principals of the agency directly, and not have his advertising handed off to a B team, get it bogged down in committee meetings, or unecessary focus groups.

Steve and I were just as capable of placing an ad in a local paper as we could Time magazine, or a professional journal for a specific product like WEI's heat sinks.

We could also be a bit more playful in some of our advertising as we did with Mi Casa Restaurant. For example, body copy that Steve wrote for "PSST! WANT TO GUACAMOLE?"

"It was during the Mexican Revolution that a Federale pilot bombed a small village with what he thought were explosives, but turned out to be a ton of ripe avocados.

All of Mexico and North America now remember this tasteful event as one of the most delicious if not messiest in current history.

Mi Casa is fortunate to have the rights to this original recipe. Now you can really guacamole the way you've always wanted to."

It is doubtful that this kind of jocular flippancy would ever have been created at your larger staid agency. New York produced several well known boutique agencies, perhaps the most memorable among them was the Della Femina & Partners Agency where Jerry Della Femina wrote an irreverent book on advertising called, *From the Wonderful Folks Who Brought You Pearl Harbor*. In the famous (or infamous) words of Jerry Della Femina, "Advertising is the most fun you can have with your clothes on."

TODAY

Advertising today is done radically differently than in our Leysen/Johnston era. Now, all an art director needs is a smart phone and a computer. Designers can knockout a half dozen logo designs in one day when it would've taken me a week. If the client doesn't like a particular color, all they have to do is make a key swipe on their laptop to change it. I would have to return to my desk, make another design in the new color, and set up another meeting for the presentation.

For me, back then, it literally was cut and paste, meaning I used scissors, X-Acto blades and rubber cement to paste-up the art for ads and brochure layouts down on illustration board, sitting at a tilt-up drafting table.

I also had to handcut amberlith overlays with an X-Acto, which were used to knock out unwanted backgrounds in photos. Staring at the red-orange plastic overlay for more than fifteen minutes made everything else look green as an after image. Again, this is a process that can easily be accomplished via the computer.

Steve would give me his typed copy that I marked-up according to my specifications regarding choice of typeface and size. This was sent by messenger to a typesetting house, and came back "camera-ready" to be pasted up along with the art.

Then it had to be photographed and turned into a photostat which could be inserted in a newspaper or magazine, or go to the printer for reproduction. If the art was full color, separations were made which meant it had to be photographed four times: In cyan, yellow, magenta, and black, which combined on the printing press made for a full-color job.

It was a very hands-on approach.

Frankly I did not adapt to the computer as a design tool.

Or to paraphrase the memorable words of Robert Duvall as Lt. Colonel Bill Kilgore in *Apocalypse Now*, "I love the smell of rubber cement in the morning. It smells like victory."

DIRECTION

An art director decided to phone his mother, and tell her what it was like to have his job at a big important agency, and all the salary he was pulling down.

"So, you're an art director," she says, "do you draw those pretty pictures in the ads?"

"No, mom, an illustrator does that."

"Oh, then you must take those photos?"

"No, we hire photographers for that."

"I see. And the words in the ad, do you write those?"

He laughed, "No, that's a job for a copywriter."

She seemed miffed. "Okay, then, you must create those logos or trademarks I see in the ads."

"No, a graphic designer does that."

"So…son, what do you do?"

"Mom, I'm an art director."

"And for that you get paid!?"

EPILOGUE

Even though Steve and I retired from advertising, we went on to seek our own independent paths in the workplace. To paraphrase Don Draper in one *Mad Men* episode when asked what he would do if he ever left Cooper/Sterling, he said, "Anything but advertising!"

Steve became a very productive freelance voice-over artist, and podcaster, while I spent twenty years teaching part-time at the university and college level, instructing in studio art and lecturing on art theory. I converted a two-car garage into a viable studio and developed a relationship with two dealers, one in Orange County, one in LA.

My abstract works have been included in numerous group and one-person exhibitions throughout Southern California, and are in private and public collections.

Steve and I meet up once or twice a year (he lives up north in Santa Clara) at our favorite coffee shop near UCI where we attempt to solve world problems.

ALSO BY MARK LEYSEN

Art Works

Once We Were Magic

The Klown

HOA**holes

Flemish Fries

Ingram Content Group UK Ltd.
Milton Keynes UK
UKHW050658060723
424521UK00004B/22

9 781088 156612